C000172271

Walking in the Clwydian Hills
and the Vale of Llangollen

World's End

Walking in the
Clwydian Hills
& the Vale of Llangollen

Carl Rogers

Mara Publications

First published in April 1995 by Mara Publications, 22 Crosland Terrace, Helsby, Warrington, Cheshire, WA6 9LY.

Second Edition published November 1997.

All enquiries regarding sales telephone: (01928) 723744

ISBN 0 9522409 3 9

> *Special thanks are due to the following individuals for checking the route descriptions: Jack and Audrey Rogers, David Telfer, Martin Ogden, Bob and Chris Nash and Richard Evans.*

© Carl Rogers 1995

All rights reserved. This publication must not be reproduced in any form without prior written permission from the publisher.

British Library Cataloguing-in-publication data.
A catalogue is available for this book from the British Library.

Whilst every effort has been made to ensure that the information in this book is correct, the author or the publisher can accept no responsibility for errors, loss or injury however caused.

Sketch maps based upon the Ordnance Survey 1:25000 Pathfinder mapping with the permission of The Controller of Her Majesty's Stationary Office. Crown Copyright 87762M.

Printed and bound by MFP Design & Print, telephone: 0161 864 4540

Contents

Location of the Walks

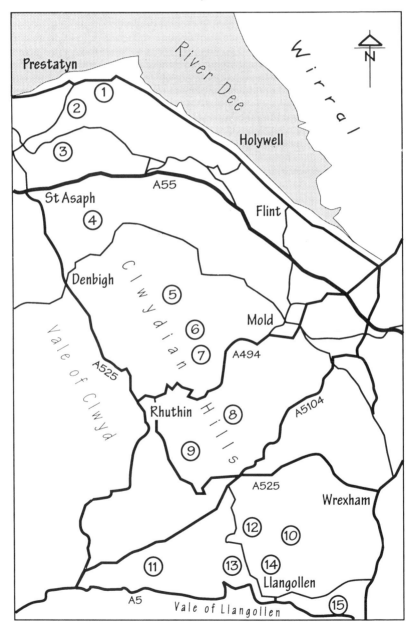

Introduction

This guide book combines two of the finest walking areas in the Welsh borders—the Clwydian Hills and the Vale of Llangollen.

The Clwydian Hills run south from Prestatyn on the North Wales coast for over 15 miles and are perhaps best known for providing either a fitting climax, or a rigorous introduction, to the 175 mile long Offa's Dyke Path which traverses the entire length of the Welsh border. Nowhere do these hills exceed 2,000 feet, but because they stand apart from their neighbours, their height and form is exaggerated and the views from their exposed summits are extensive. This is particularly true to the west where the panorama takes in the Vale of Clwyd and the distant peaks of Snowdonia.

The Vale of Llangollen, overlooked by the beautiful Llantysilio Hills and the dramatic limestone escarpment of Eglwyseg Mountain, is considered by many to be one of the loveliest valleys in Wales. Deeply cut and often wooded, it provides one of the few major routes through the Welsh hills and has long been used as a gateway to North Wales. As a result, the valley is steeped in history and has many relics from its troubled past.

For the walker, an extensive and well maintained network of public footpaths and bridleways give easy access to this beautiful landscape and few problems should be experienced by those following the routes outlined in the following pages. Footpaths used by Offa's Dyke Path are particularly well defined although there is ample scope for getting away from the crowds and you are likely to have the lesser known footpaths to yourself.

History

From the earliest times Britain has seen a succession of immigrant peoples who have moved north and west across the island either absorbing earlier inhabitants or forcing them into remoter regions. The last of these westward migrations in the prehistoric period involved the Iron Age or Celtic tribes who began to settle in Britain from about 500 BC onwards. It was these tribes who built the line of hill forts which crown many summits in the Clwydian Hills today and faced the Romans armies of Julius Caesar in 49 CE.

The ruins of Castell Dinas Bran

The Romans quickly subdued the tribes of southern Britain, but those who refused to submit to their rule fled west. One of the most colourful characters from this period is Prince Caratacus or Caradog who led the western tribes of the Silures and the Ordovices in a guerilla war against the might of Rome along what is now the Welsh border. He was eventually betrayed by his own people and taken captive to Rome. Under Roman rule Britain was to remain relatively peaceful for almost 300 years.

When the Romans withdrew from Britain they left behind a political vacuum. The kingdom lay undefended and suffered attacks from all sides. Irish tribesmen began to invade the west coast, Germanic tribes were harassing the east and Picts from beyond Hadrian's Wall were making raids into what is now northern England. The king of Britain at this time was the enigmatic character known as Vortigern. Little is known about him, but he is generally given the blame for the Saxon colonisation of England in the fifth century. It is said that in an attempt to control the attacks on his kingdom he enlisted the help of Saxon mercenaries from the continent. At first this was successful, but the Saxons soon turned on their employer, took lands for themselves and began establishing their own kingdoms. This led to fierce conflict with the British but the Saxon colonisation could not be stopped. The whole of eastern Britain soon came under their control and by the close of the sixth century, the British tribes who survived were confined mainly to what is now Wales, Cornwall, Cumbria and Strathclyde.

During this period, an army from the Saxon kingdom of Northumbria gained a great victory against the Celts in 616 near Chester. This effectively severed the British who occupied what is now Wales, from their kinsmen in northern Britain and Cornwall, confining them to the land that would become Wales and caused them to develop as a separate people. From this time on, they began to call themselves

'Cymry' or 'fellow countrymen'. The division between the Cymry and the Saxons of England was dictated mainly by geography and lay approximately on the line of the present border of Wales. For the next 600 years there would be little peace along this new borderland territory.

Unlike the Romans, the Saxons were unable to completely conquer the Welsh and advanced little beyond the present border. The difficult mountain terrain probably enabled the Welsh to retain both their lands and their identity when other British tribes eventually disappeared. For this reason Offa, the eighth century ruler of the kingdom of Mercia (the area we now know as the Midlands), satisfied himself by confining the Welsh to this highland region with his great earthwork a few miles to the west of the present border.

When William the Conqueror defeated the Saxon king Harold in 1066, a new menace presented itself across the border. The Normans were the most organised and powerful fighting forced of their day and they were not content to let the unconquered Welsh live peacefully beyond Offa's Dyke. They tackled the problem of the Welsh by giving lands along the border to powerful barons who had a free reign to attack and plunder Welsh kingdoms in order to increase their own lands and power. They became known as Marcher Lords and caused the Welsh endless trouble during the early Middle Ages. Sadly, many were able to exploit rivalry between Welsh princes who often allied themselves with the English to increase their own power.

One of the most famous battles from this period was the victory won by Owain Gwynedd against Henry II on the slopes of the Berwyns between Corwen and Glyn Ceiriog in 1169. Henry had become concerned at the alliance Owain had made with Rhys ap Gruffydd of Deheubarth and gathered a huge army to destroy them. Owain waited at Corwen while Henry approached by means of Glyn Ceiriog, which involved a march over the high tops of the Berwyn mountains. Henry's army was harassed by Welsh archers as he made slow progress along the thickly wooded Ceiriog valley and the king was almost killed in one skirmish at Bronygarth near Chirk. In the end however, it was the appalling Welsh weather that defeated Henry's army. Heavy rain and strong winds forced him into a humiliating retreat without even engaging the main Welsh forces.

In the following century the rise of Llywelyn Fawr and the prominence of his grandson Llywelyn ap Gruffydd ('Llywelyn the Last') led to Wales' final war with England. Edward I succeeded his farther Henry III in 1277 and at his coronation he demanded the attendance of Prince Llywelyn to swear allegiance. When Llywelyn refused both to attend the coronation and swear allegiance to Edward, war broke out. Edward invaded North Wales from Chester and sent a fleet of ships to Anglesey to seize the crops on which the Welsh were so dependant. Llywelyn was cornered and compelled to surrender.

Eliseg's Pillar

At the Treaty of Rhuddlan Llywelyn lost most of his lands retaining only Snowdonia and Anglesey. His brother Dafydd, who had fought for Edward against Llywelyn, was given rulership of the lands between the Conwy and the Dee. Ironically, it was Dafydd who triggered the final rebellion against Edward. He resented the interference of English officials left behind by the crown and called to his brother Llywelyn for help. Llywelyn answered the call and the two soon took control of the nearby castles at Harwarden, Ruthin and Hope. Support for the rising was great at first but Edward was a powerful opponent and the chances of complete success were never great. The end came with Llywelyn's death in a minor skirmish near Builth Wells. Dafydd declared himself Prince of Wales and continued the fight but was eventually handed over to the English by his own people. Edward considered him a traitor and condemned him to death at Shrewsbury where he suffered a terrible execution, being hung drawn and quartered in 1283.

The final conflict between Wales and England came over a century later with the rebellion of Owain Glyndwr in 1400. He came from Glyn Dyfrdwy at the foot of the Llantysilio hills and was well into middle age when his rise to fame began. Support for the rebellion was great at first and he was soon declared 'Prince of Wales' by his countrymen. Even today he is remembered as one of the great national heroes of Wales, but his victory was short lived—little more than nine years. This brought an end to conflict between the Welsh and English, although the present boundary was not formalised for another century and a half. This came with the Tudor Acts of Union in 1536 and 1542.

Today this border region is as peaceful and unspoilt as anywhere in Britain, although castle ruins and old town fortifications remain to remind us of more troubled times.

Visible remains of area's history are perhaps most outstanding in the Llangollen area where one of the most important Dark Age monuments in the whole of Wales can be seen—Eliseg's Pillar. The pillar is in fact the shaft of a ninth century inscribed stone cross which commemorates Eliseg, Prince of Powys, a contemporary of Offa (see chapter 13). Nearby are the thirteenth century ruins of Valle Crucis Abbey, founded by Madog ap Gruffydd whose father is thought to have been responsible for building Castell Dinas Bran. The scant remains of this fortress crown the summit of a green conical hill which overlooks the town of Llangollen and provide what must be one of the most romantic settings for a castle anywhere in the country.

The earliest remains to be seen are probably the Iron Age hillforts which crown several summits in the Clwydian Hills. The most extensive of these is visited on walk number 5 where extensive earthworks enclose an area of over 50 acres. The ramparts are so prominent that they have given the hill its name, Penycloddiau which means "hill of the trenches". Other notable examples can be seen on Foel Fenlli and Moel Arthur.

Maps

For those interested in further exploration, the Ordnance Survey Pathfinder maps are recommended. These have a scale of 1:25,000 (approximately 2½ inches to 1 mile) and show every field, wood, stream and building, along with public rights of way information printed in green.

For less detailed work the Landranger series are excellent. These maps are produced to a scale of 1:50,000 (approximately 1¼ inches to 1 mile) and are ideal for locating the start of each walk. Sheet numbers are given at the beginning of each route.

Glossary of Welsh names

Aber ....*river mouth*

Afon ....*river*

Alt ....*hillside*

Bach ....*little*

Bryn ....*hill, eminence*

Cae ....*field, enclosure*

Caer ....*fort*

Canol ....*centre*

Capel ....*chapel*

Carn, Carnedd ...*heap of stones*

Carreg ....*crag or stone*

Castell ....*castle*

Cefn ....*ridge*

Clogwyn ....*cliff*

Clwyd ....*gate*

Coch ....*red*

Coed ....*wood*

Cors ....*bog or swamp*

Craig ....*crag*

Crib ....*jagged ridge*

Croes ....*cross*

Cwm ....*coombe*

Dinas ....*city, fortress*

Ddu ....*black*

Dyffryn ....*valley*

Eglwys ....*church*

Eryri ....*highland*

Esgair ....*ridge*

Fach ....*small*

Faes ....*meadow*

Fawr ....*large*

Felin ....*mill*

Ffordd ....*road*

Ffynnon ....*well or fountain*

Foel ....*bare hill*

Gaer ....*camp*

Galt ....*slope*

Garn ....*an eminence*

Glas ....*blue-green*

Glyn ....*deep valley*

Goch ....*red*

Gors ....*swamp*

Grach ....*scabby*

Groes ....*cross*

Gwern ....*alder coppice*

Gwyn ....*white*

Hafod ....*summer dwelling*

Hen ....*old*

Isaf ....*lower*

Llan ....*church*

Llyn ....*lake*

Llys ....*hall or court*

Lon ....*lane*

Maen ....*stone*

Maes ....*field or meadow*

Mawr ....*large*

Moel ....*rounded hill*

Mor ....*sea*

Mynach ....*monk*

Mynydd ....*mountain*

Newydd ....*new*

Ogof ....*cave*

Pant ....*hollow*

Parc ....*park*

Pen ....*head or point*

Penrhyn ....*promontory*

Pentre ....*village*

Pistyll ....*waterfall*

Plas ....*house*

Pont ....*bridge*

Pwll ....*pool*

Rhos............................*moorland*

Rhyd ....*ford*

Sarn ....*causeway*

Tomen ....*mound*

Tref ....*town*

Twll ....*cavern*

Twr ....*tower*

Ty ....*house*

Tyddyn ....*farmstead*

Uchaf ....*upper*

Waun ....*moorland*

Wen ....*white*

Wern ....*alder swamp*

Y, Yr ....*the*

Yn ....*in*

Ynys ....*island*

1. Gronant

Distance: *4¾ miles.*

Start: Begin near the Gronant Inn in the village of Gronant 1½ miles east of Prestatyn, just south of the A548.
Grid ref. 093 831 (Landranger 116, Pathfinder 737).

The Route

1. From the Gronant Inn turn right along the road and just beyond the war memorial, steps and a small gate lead into fields on the left. Bear diagonally-right through the field to a stile which leads into a large wood. Follow the path through the trees and join a prominent track which rises to the left. A stile straight ahead at the top of the rise leads out of the trees and into fields. Cut straight through a small field to a stile, then bear right along the fence and contour the hillside for some distance.

A fine view of the coast now begins to open out. Behind, the Hilbre Islands and the northern tip of Wirral are visible with the Lancashire coast on the skyline. Straight ahead, the North Wales coast curves west towards the Great Orme with the mountains of Snowdonia on the horizon.

Today, this coastal plain is heavily developed and the new A55 coast road brings tourists and holiday makers from nearby Merseyside to a line of resorts from Rhyl to Caernarfon. During the Middle Ages less welcome visitors came this way in the form of Saxon and Norman invaders. Before them came the Romans under general Suetonius, who led his armies from Chester to Anglesey (about AD 61) and slaughtered the Druid priesthood on the shores of the Menai Strait.

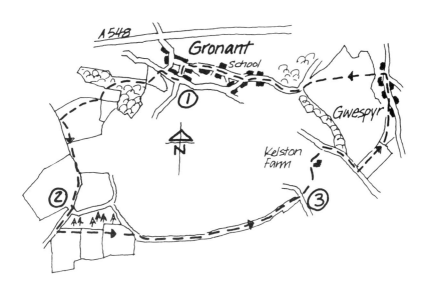

Generations of Welsh leaders fought against these invaders, but defeat finally came at the hands of Edward I in 1283. Edward followed up his conquest by building a line of castles along the North Wales coast to maintain control of the Welsh.

The sovereignty of Wales was not the only cause fought for on these lands though. In 1399 the fate of the English crown was decided on the dull coastal plain near Penmaenrhos when, on his approach to Rhuddlan Castle, Richard II was betrayed by the Earl of Northumberland. This allowed Henry Bolingbroke to seize the crown and become Henry IV of England.

This act caused great resentment among the Welsh, most of whom had been happy with Richard as king. In the years that followed, this resentment overflowed into overwhelming support for the rebellion of Owain Glyndwr. It was Henry's favour for Lord Grey of Ruthin (in a relatively minor boundary dispute with Glyndwr) which triggered the famous rebellion.

Somewhere along this coast between Prestatyn and the Great Orme lies the wreck of Britain's first submarine, the 'Resurgam', which sank while being towed to Portsmouth in February 1880. It was designed and built by Reverend William Garrett, a Liverpool curate.

On the hills above Gronant

At a fence which runs directly up the hillside, turn left and rise to join a faint track where the slope eases. The track soon disappears but the right of way continues along the field edge towards a mast at the top of the hill.

2. Enter a rough lane beside the mast and bear right for about 300 yards. Just beyond a small conifer wood, a stile on the left leads into fields once more. Bear half-left along the field edge and follow the path through several fields following a line of stiles to enter a green lane with a small pond to the right. Turn right and follow the lane for almost 1 mile.

Ahead, a wide panorama opens out which takes in almost all of western Wirral from the Hilbre islands and beaches at West Kirby, to the dried out seaports which flourished during the sixteenth and seventeenth centuries at Parkgate and Neston. Today, grass and saltmarsh surround the old quays and the nearby villages have remained small and rural. Beyond Wirral, the industrial activities of a later age have produced the chimneys and flares at Stanlow on the shores of the River Mersey.

To the southeast, the northern end of the Mid Cheshire Ridge at Helsby and Frodsham can just be seen, while Moel Famau marks the highest point on the Clwydian Hills to the south. On exceptionally clear days the Isle of Man may just be visible over 70 miles away.

3. At a T junction turn right, then immediately left over a stile and follow the field edge to Kelston Farm. The right of way has been diverted right around the farmyard and down the driveway to Llanasa Road.

Turn right along the road and after about 400 yards turn left through a kissing gate onto a field path. Follow the path beside the wall for some distance, eventually bearing right to the road opposite the Masons Arms public house in the village of Gwespyr. Turn left down the hill and follow the road through the village.

Just beyond Delyn Metals, a large scrap metal yard on the left, turn left onto a signed footpath. After a stile the right of way cuts straight through a large open field keeping to the right of a small group of trees.

Below us on the coast lie the holiday developments at Gronant and Prestatyn which developed during the late nineteenth century when this coast provided sought after holiday retreats for the high populations of industrial Merseyside. This was the heyday of seaside resorts and a string of towns developed all along this coast. The most famous of these is Rhyl which still attracts numerous visitors to its pleasure beach, discos and fairgrounds.

There is little of historic interest at Gronant and Prestatyn today although there are traces of a Norman motte and bailey castle at Prestatyn, along with the remains of a Roman bathhouse uncovered 1930s.

The right of way across the field is just visible on the ground and aims almost directly towards Gronant village to join the access road to Talacre Abbey. A kissing gate leads onto the road with a small lodge to the right. Turn left here and follow the road to the outskirts of Gronant.

Where the road bends left, bear right onto a path which runs beside gardens with Gronant CP School on the right. Continue straight ahead at an estate road and follow a second footpath behind gardens, before bearing left to the road. Turn right here and after about 200 yards, bear left into Llys Dewi, a small cul-de-sac with a footpath at its head. This brings you once more to the Gronant Inn.

2. Gwaenysgor

Distance: *5½ miles.*

Start: Begin the walk from the little green in the centre of the village where there is a small information board outlining points of interest.
Grid ref. 075 811 (Landranger 116, Pathfinder 737).

The Route

1. From the village centre head north along the Prestatyn road and after about 50 yards turn left into an access road with white stone cottages on either side. At the end of the road and beyond the last house on the right, the lane continues as a footpath contained by hedges. After a stile the path bends left and enters an open field. A little further on you reach the edge of the hillside overlooking Meliden and Prestatyn. A stile and finger post indicate that you have joined Offa's Dyke path. Turn left here and follow the well worn footpath which gradually descends to a finger post.

Despite their modern appearance, both Meliden and Prestatyn are ancient settlements of Anglo-Saxon origin. They originate from a time of Saxon advance into Welsh territories, possibly during the seventh and eight centuries, although this would always have been a dangerous frontier territory for those early settlers. Evidence for this can be seen in the nearby earthworks of Off's Dyke and the earlier Watt's Dyke (both east of here) built to defend the border with Wales.

Meliden developed rapidly during the eighteenth century as a centre for lead mining and remains of this industry can still be seen in the hills at the back of the town. The nearby Fish Mine was so named because the spoil heaps formed the shape of a fish.

The name Prestatyn has been corrupted from a name similar to that of Preston in Lancashire and is evidence of the constant change in control of the area between the English and Welsh prior to Edward I's conquest of Wales in the thirteenth century. There are many other examples of Anglicised Welsh names and the Welsh spelling of names which are of Anglo-Saxon origin along the border which originate from this period.

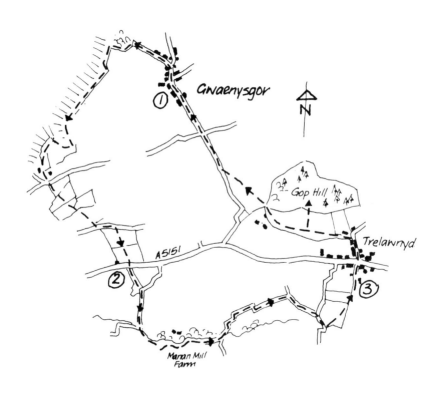

The modern from of Prestatyn came into being during the nineteenth century when the town developed as a tourist destination where visitors could come and sample the sea and mountain air from the nearby industrial towns around Merseyside and Manchester. The coming of the railways in the mid century brought North Wales within easy reach of many thousands of trippers and a string of resorts developed all along this coast to cater for the new trade. Rhyl is of course the most well known of these resorts and remains the most popular.

Keep left at the finger post ("Bryniau") ignoring the path to "Bishopswood" on the right. A little further on the path passes along the top of a quarry on the right before entering trees. Turn right at a T junction here taking the signed path to "Bryniau" once more. Beyond the trees, a stile leads into a field; keep left and follow the obvious path (marked with the Offa's Dyke Path symbol) to an access road with a house to the right ("Red Roofs"). Turn left and walk away from the house to join a quiet lane. Turn left here, then left again after a few yards. About 50 yards further on, look for a stile and sign on the right beside the driveway to "Clarence House".

The right of way through the following fields is well walked and well worn. After the final field a line of wooden steps takes you down the bank and into a quiet lane. Turn left along the lane and after about 200 yards, turn right into fields again by a stile and sign. Walk directly through the centre of a large field to a stile beside a gate. Take a direct line through the following field keeping to the left of a large farm.

2. Cross the A5151 and walk down a broad farm track almost opposite to enter a quiet lane once again. Bear right and walk along the lane until it bends very sharply to the right. Keep left here (straight ahead!) and follow an access road to a T junction with a large house ("Felin Fawr") directly ahead. Take the left turn here (Offa's Dyke Path bears right at this point) which will take you for some distance along an unmade road. Where this bears left to a house, continue straight ahead on the obvious footpath. At a T junction turn left and follow the sunken lane for almost ½ mile. This can be very wet near the stream.

At the next T junction turn right and continue to the lane. Turn right along the lane and just before the bend bear left onto a short section of old road before turning left onto a signed field path. Walk directly through the centre of a large field with the cairn on the summit of Gop Hill directly ahead. Aim for the top right-hand corner of the field where you will find a stile partly hidden in the hedge. In the following field keep right along the hedge and after about 50 yards cross a stile on the right. Turn left now and continue on the opposite side of the fence to join an access road near cottages on the left.

3. Walk along the access road to the main road (A5151) in the centre of Trelawnyd. Turn right and after a few yards cross over taking the signed "Llanasa" road on the left. Walk up the hill but before the right-hand bend at the top of the rise, turn left into a short access road with a well hidden footpath sign. Beyond the final house a stone stile takes you into a large field on the lower slopes of Gop Hill. Contour the hillside keeping to the obvious footpath. Partway along the path, a finger post indicates a permissive footpath to the summit of Gop Hill. If you visit the summit return to this point to continue the walk.

Gop Hill is famous for the large prehistoric drystone cairn crowning its summit. This curious cone can be seen for several miles and is over 60 feet high making it the largest of its kind in Wales.

At the far end of the field, keep right above farm buildings and look for a stile in the corner of the field below woods on

Field path below Gop Hill

the right. Walk directly through the following field aiming just to the left of Gwaenysgor in the distance. Cross a stile in the far fence, then bear half-left to a second stile in the corner which leads into a quiet lane. Turn right now and follow the lane back to Gwaenysgor keeping straight ahead at the crossroads.

Gwaenysgor is an attractive unspoilt village with many fine old buildings. The information board sited on the green in the village centre gives details of the best examples.

The unusual name of this village is thought to mean "the meadow of the camp" from gwaun "meadow" and ysgor "camp or fortification". This could be a reference to the remains on Gop Hill or even to the northern limit of Offa's Dyke which may have ended somewhere near here. There is much controversy about exactly where the dyke finished or if it ever was after Offa's death at Rhuddlan in AD 796.

3. Cwm

Distance: *3 or 4¾ miles.*

Start: Begin at the village of Cwm, 1 mile south of Dyserth. Park near the Blue Lion Inn.
Grid ref. 066 774 (Landranger 116, Pathfinder 755).

The Route

1. Walk up the lane past the Blue Lion Inn and the church and after about 300 yards, turn right (gate) into fields opposite a white cottage. Keep to the field edge in the first field then, after crossing the stream and stile, rise diagonally-right through the following field to a quiet lane.

Turn left along the lane and after about 400 yards, look for a signed footpath on the right. Turn sharp right onto this path and make your way through a recently felled woodland. Just before the top of the hill look for a waymark which directs you left onto a more gentle woodland path. At the top of the rise climb over a stile and walk along the edge of the woods with fields to the left.

A gate leads onto a track which immediately bends left; follow the track to a lane. Turn left here and after a few yards turn right into fields where a stile and sign indicating Offa's Dyke Path, mark the continuation of the right of way. The path, now much more obvious, runs beside the hedge before bearing left to cross a quiet lane by two stiles. Bear half-left through the field now passing between stone cottages to a lane at the hamlet of Marian Cwm.

Almost opposite and a little to the left, the path continues over Marian Ffrith, a rounded sheep grazed hill with a fine

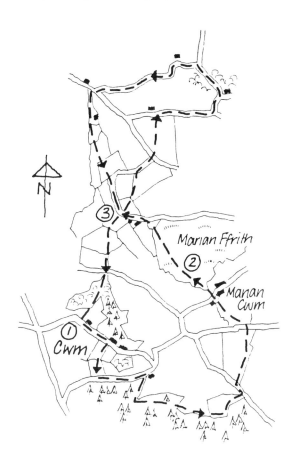

panorama from the top. Bear half-left up the gentle slopes
and look for waymarks which indicate the right of way.

*The view from this little hilltop is extensive and takes in much
of the Vale of Clwyd laid out like a vast green carpet with the dark
serrated skyline of Snowdonia in the distance. The coastal resorts
from Rhyl to Llandudno can be seen lining the bay to the northwest,
while below us on the east bank of Afon Clwyd stands the town of
Rhuddlan.*

Today, this rather ordinary town gives little impression of its importance during the Middle Ages when it played a key role in the Welsh Wars. It developed around the castle built by Edward I in 1277 at the head of what was then a large tidal estuary. This site enabled the castle to be supplied by shipping during a siege, a feature Edward incorporated into all his Welsh castles.

The fact that Edward chose Rhuddlan as a key site in his conquest of Wales was no accident. To the southeast of the present castle a mound, known as Twthill, is known to be the site of an earlier fortress and there was a second stronghold at nearby Dyserth, destroyed by Prince Llywelyn in 1263.

These earlier castles were used by a number of English kings including Harold, William the Conqueror, Henry II and King John, who all launched campaigns against the Welsh from here. The crossing of Afon Clwyd had been difficult to hold ever since the English won the Battle of Rhuddlan in 796 and it was here that Offa, one of the most famous rulers of the Dark Ages and builder of the nearby earthwork which bears his name, reputedly met his end in 798.

Edward's conquest of Wales began shortly after his succession to the throne of England in 1272 while on crusade. In 1274 he held a belated coronation at which he demanded the attendance of both the King of Scotland and the Prince of Wales, at that time the powerful leader Llywelyn ap Gruffydd. Llywelyn, who had recently uncovered a plot to assassinate him by his brother Dafydd, refused to attend and when Edward welcomed Dafydd to his court, Llywelyn also refused to pay the levy of 3,000 marks paid annually to the English crown.

Edward saw this as outright rebellion and, having launched an attack from Chester, gained Rhuddlan in a decisive battle in 1277. He immediate began work on a new castle and soon moved his headquarters from Chester to Rhuddlan. From here Edward launched attacks by sea along the coast and forced Llywelyn into the mountains of Snowdonia. When threatened by starvation, Llywelyn surrendered and at the treaty of Rhuddlan in 1277 lost all his lands except the heartland of Gwynedd west of Afon Conwy. His brother Dafydd, who had fought on Edward's side, was given overlordship of the lands between Afon Conwy and the River Dee.

Ironically, it was Dafydd who began the next rebellion against Edward. He resented the interference of English officials left behind at Rhuddlan and called to Llywelyn for help. Llywelyn answered the call and the castles at Harwarden, Ruthin and Hope soon fell to the Welsh. Independence looked hopeful for a while but Llywelyn and Dafydd were now defending their recently recovered kingdom from attacks on several fronts.

The end came when Llywelyn was killed after he became isolated from his army and ran into a small band of English soldiers who failed to recognise him. His head was cut off and sent to Edward who had it displayed at the Tower of London. Dafydd now declared himself Prince of Wales but was reputedly handed over to the English by his own men shortly afterwards. Edward condemned him to a terrible traitors death at Shrewsbury in October 1283. He was dragged through the streets before being hung, drawn and then beheaded before his body was quartered. Dafydd's head was also displayed at the Tower of London alongside that of his brother Llywelyn.

The present ruinous state of Rhuddlan Castle is the result of demolition at the hands of Parliamentarians during the Civil War.

Inland to the northeast you will see the curious cone of Gop Hill crowned by the largest prehistoric cairn in Wales. The cairn is over 60 feet high and formed entirely of drystone mounding. On the southern slopes of the hill are to be found the most northerly signs of Offa's Dyke, leading to the conclusion that it was never finished following Offa's death. Its proposed line is thought to have ended at either Prestatyn or Rhuddlan.

29

Following Offa's Dyke Path to Marian Ffrith

2. Follow the right of way over the hilltop bearing left to a stone stile in the corner of the field. Pass through a small field and turn left along a farm track. About 100 yards beyond the farmhouse turn right over a stone stile and cut through the centre of a small field. (For a shorter round turn left off the track instead of right and continue from point **3**)

In the following field bear left along the hedge to a stile which leads onto a track and turn right. At the road turn left then, after about 20 yards, the path continues through a large field on the right (stile). After a smaller field a stile leads onto a bridleway; turn right now and follow the bridleway for some distance.

Beyond a stream bear left onto a white track and at the road bear left again. Follow the road for some distance.

At a T junction turn right and look for a signed footpath on the left by some old farm buildings. This is a narrow enclosed footpath which rises to a tarmac access road. Turn right here and just before the house, the path bears right up the gorse covered bank to a stile just beyond the outbuildings. Follow a line of stiles through the following fields to a track and turn right.

3. About 100 yards before a farmhouse, turn right over a stile (Offa's Dyke Path turns left here) and cut through the field to a stile beside a gate. In the following field bear half-left in the direction of a wooded hillside and cross the remains of a stile to the right of a gate. Keep to the field edge now and enter a quiet lane. Opposite, the right of way drops between hedges into Church Wood.

Follow the path through the trees trending rightwards to a stile which leads into fields just above the Blue Lion Inn. Cut through the field to a footpath sign beside the church. Return along the lane to point **1.**

4. Tremeirchion

Distance: *4½ miles*

Start: Begin the walk in the village of Tremeirchion, 1½ miles south of Rhuallt on the B5429. Park in the village and start at the Salusbury Arms public house.
Grid ref. 083 730 (Landranger 116, Pathfinder 755).

The Route

1. Walk up the lane past the Salusbury Arms and look for a footpath on the right just beyond a farm. Bear half-left across the field to enter a green lane by a large house (Cae-gwyn). Turn right then left over a stile after a few yards, signposted "Craig Tremeirchion". Descend the field with Cae-gwyn to your left and after a stile drop into a small bracken covered valley following the path beside the stream. Cross two footbridges on the left and bear right up the bank following the waymarks to enter a lane by a white cottage on the left ("Craig Bach"). Turn right and follow the lane down the hill for some distance.

2. Where the lane bends sharp right, bear left over a stile, signposted "Y Graig, Bodfari". Enter the woods of Y Graig Nature Reserve, an area of woodland and limestone outcrops purchased by North Wales Naturalists Trust in 1987. Ignoring signs to "The Summit" and "Quarry" on either side, continue straight ahead through the woods. As you break out of the trees fine views open out.

The green sweep of the Vale of Clwyd now opens out below, a landscape of farmland and villages reaching north to the coast at Rhyl. Although a picture of peace and tranquillity today, this has not always been the case, for it was here that Prince Llywelyn and his brother *Dafydd began their final revolt against Edward I in the thirteenth century.*

Dafydd had been given lands at nearby Denbigh in 1277 prior to his final conflict with Edward which resulted in Llywelyn's death in a minor skirmish near Builth Wells and Dafydd's brutal execution as a traitor at Shrewsbury in 1282.

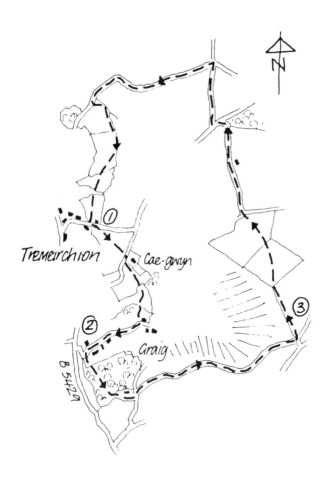

His lands at Denbigh were given to Henry de Lacy, Earl of Lincoln and it was at this time that Denbigh castle and town walls were built in order to hold the area in subjection to the English crown. Work on the defences was halted in 1294 when Welsh rebels captured the town but the rising was short lived and de Lacy was able to continue the work which was still unfinished when he died in 1311.

Despite the strong defences, the town suffered destruction twice during the fifteenth century. First during the uprising of Owain Glyndwr in 1402 and again by Jasper Tudor, Earl of Pembroke in 1468, while the castle was in the hands of the Yorkists during the Wars of the Roses.

During the Civil War the castle was held by Royalists and Charles I stayed there for a few days in 1645. A year later it was surrendered to Parliamentarians who carried out the usual destruction reducing it to the ruins which we see today. The castle and walls are now open to the public.

As the path bears left up the hill turn right over a stile and walk along a narrow footpath to join a track. Turn right along the track and at a T junction turn left. After a few yards turn right and follow a narrow rising lane for almost 1 mile.

Looking back from the upper part of the lane there is a wide view of the northern end of the Vale of Clwyd. Prominent is the tiny cathedral of St Asaph siting boldly in the position which, for almost 1,000 years, earned it the reputation for being the most frequently destroyed religious building in Wales.

This exposed location on the north coast left St Asaph mercilessly open to attacks from across the Irish Sea throughout the Dark Ages. Speaking about this period Michael Senior in his book, "Portrait of North Wales" says: "It seems every time anyone invaded North Wales they paused to burn down St Asaph cathedral." As a result, when Edward I tried to move the diocese to Rhuddlan where he had recently built his new castle, he was heavily supported by the bishop and his cannons.

St Asaph did not just suffer destruction at the hands of those who came across the sea though. In the early fifteenth century Owain Glyndwr, hailed by his countrymen as the new "Prince of Wales", also put the cathedral to the torch along with much of nearby Ruthin and Denbigh.

3. At the top of the rise go through a gate into the lane and turn left immediately onto Offa's Dyke Path (sign). This rises along field edges until, after a second stile at the top of the rise, you bear diagonally-right through the field to a stile in the fence. Drop through the following field to the corner of a quiet lane.

Follow the lane straight ahead and at a T junction turn left. After a few yards turn right into a second lane and at the top of the rise turn left onto a bridleway, signposted "Offa's Dyke". Follow the bridleway which shortly descends the hillside ignoring a path on the right at the foot of the slope. A few yards beyond this join a tarmac lane and about 250 yards further on, opposite a stone house ("Ty Cerrig"), turn left through a gate (footpath sign). Pass the outbuildings and cross the stream before bearing half-right up the field keeping to field edges.

After a stile drop to a second stream then bear half-right up the field and follow a line of stiles through the following fields to emerge in the lane beside the Salusbury Arms once more.

5. Penycloddiau & Moel Arthur

Distance: *6 or 7¾ miles*

Start: Begin the walk at Llangwyfan Forestry car park situated at the highest point of the lane which runs between Llangwyfan and Nannerch.
Grid ref. 139 668 (Landranger 116, Pathfinder 772).

The Route

1. From the little car park follow Offa's Dyke Path northwards into the plantations. Immediately you are presented with three forestry tracks; take the right-hand track for a few yards before bearing right onto a much narrower, though well used footpath which runs along the very edge of the trees. Just before the earthworks which encircle the hilltop of Penycloddiau, turn right over a stile and follow the signed footpath to the summit cairn at the northern end of the enclosure.

The earthworks which encircle the summit form the largest Iron Age enclosure on the Clwydian Hills. In all, over 50 acres lie within its triple banks which are still remarkably well preserved. The earthworks are such a prominent feature of the hilltop that they have given it its name—Penycloddiau means "hill of the trenches".

Thankfully the nearby conifer plantations of the Llangwyfan Forest have stopped short of the summit enclosure enabling the walker to enjoy extensive views over the Vale of Clwyd in fine weather. If you are lucky you will be able to see the distant peaks of Snowdonia rising above the Denbigh Moors.

2. From the summit follow the Offa's Dyke Path northwards out of the enclosure and across the open moor to the pass at 1,004 feet. Turn sharp left here onto a farm track which contours the hillside for about 2 miles.

If your walk along the exposed ridge was windy you will be better able to enjoy the views westwards to the Vale of Clwyd from the relative shelter of this lower path.

As you leave the woods at Nant Simon, look for a path which veers left just before a gate. If you want to cut short

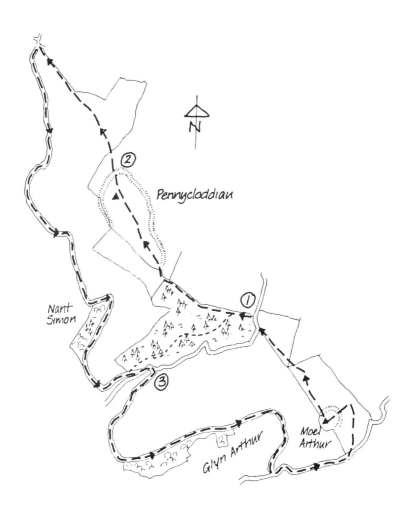

the walk, follow this path back to the car park at point **1**. For a longer round, continue through the gate and follow the track a road.

3. Turn left along the road and just beyond a sharp right-hand bend, turn right onto a second track. This contours the hillside for some distance to join the hill road above Glyn Arthur (about 1½ miles).

Turn left along the road and continue to the little car park at the top of the pass where you rejoin the Offa's Dyke Path on the left. Make a short steep ascent aiming for a broad shoulder to the right of the summit of Moel Arthur. At the top of the rise a path on the left leads through heather to the exposed summit.

Like Penycloddiau, this hilltop is crowned by the earthworks of an Iron Age hill fort built over 2,000 years ago by Celts of the Deceangli tribe who inhabited this part of Wales in the years before the Roman invasion.

At almost 1,500 feet the view is extensive and you are treated to a bird's eye view of the Vale of Clwyd. Eastwards, you will be able to pick out the long arm of the Wirral Peninsula with the hills between Beeston and Frodsham rising from the Cheshire Plain. To the south, the summit cone of Moel Famau, highest point on the Clwydian Hills, rises above the surrounding moors, while the distant peaks of the Arans fill the skyline to the southwest.

From here continue northwards to rejoin the main Offa's Dyke Path near a stile which leads into grazing fields. Follow the obvious path through sloping fields to the road. Turn right here and the forestry car park lies a few yards away.

6. Moel Famau from Cilcain

Distance: *5½ miles*

Start: Begin in the little village of Cilcain, 3 miles north of Loggerheads. Park near the church and the White Horse Inn. *Grid ref. 177 652 (Landranger 116, Pathfinder 772).*

The Route

1. Turn left just beyond the church and follow the lane out of the village with the curving hillside of Moel Famau directly ahead. After a short steep descent the lane bears sharp left; turn right here onto a farm track, then immediately left through a gate ("Tyddyn-y-Foel"). After about 20 yards a stile on the right leads into fields. Follow the right of way along field edges until a stile leads into a green lane. Go straight ahead here and follow a rising track which becomes a little less distinct beyond a gate.

After about ½ mile, make a steep rise up open heather covered slopes before the angle eases near the corner of a conifer plantation on the left. Continue straight ahead here with the woods to your left and make one final rise to the summit.

From the summit there is a wide panorama, particularly west across the wide expanse of the Vale of Clwyd where the little market town of Ruthin sits comfortably amid green fields. Further west, the high land of the Denbigh Moors has been covered on this eastern side by the dark green conifers of the Clocaenog Forest, while the peaks of Snowdonia peep over the horizon.

To the north the radio mast at Moel y Parc is visible, while the Iron Age hillforts on Moel Arthur and Penycloddiau, provide land marks from an earlier age. To the south, the rolling tops of the

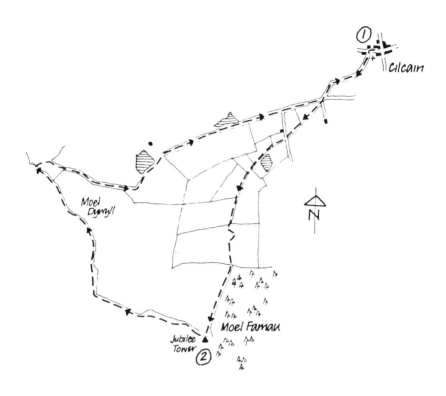

Clwydian Hills dissolve into the shapeless moors of Llandegla before the Llantysilio Hills rise again to the west. To the east lies the flatness of the Cheshire Plain and the Deeside and Merseyside industrial belts.

The ruined tower which crowns the highest point was built in 1810 to commemorate the 50th year of the reign of King George III. It was originally designed in the Egyptian style to reach a height of 150 feet, but the plans were never fully carried out and the structure that was built collapsed in 1862 following a series of gales. Attempts to restore the tower for Queen Victoria's Golden Jubilee in 1887 were a failure and the modest structure which we now see is all that remains.

2. From the Jubilee Tower follow Offa's Dyke Path north towards the rounded bulk of Moel Dywyll.

Beyond Moel Dywyll, drop to a little pass where a track crosses the hills between Cilcain and Llangynhafal. Turn right through the gate (signposted "Cilcain 2.5 m") and follow the track for about 200 yards before bearing right onto a signed path which runs between stone walls towards a small reservoir. Keep to the right of the reservoir ignoring all other footpaths and join the access road just below the dam.

Turn right here and follow the road for about 1 mile. At the lane turn left and return to Cilcain.

Approaching the summit of Moel Famau

7. Moel Famau & Foel Fenlli

Distance: *3½ or 6¼ miles.*

Start: Begin at the forest car park situated one mile along the narrow lane which leaves the A494 Mold to Ruthin road, about ½ mile west of Loggerheads.
Grid ref. 172 611 (Landranger 116, Pathfinder 772 & 788).

The Route

1. There are two car parks and a WC block here. Begin at the roofed information board between the two car parks where a well worn footpath (rather than a forestry track) rises beside the stream. Where a forestry track crosses the path, bear left and at a junction of tracks, continue straight ahead following a steeper footpath. After a short stiff pull the angle eases and walking becomes easier. Follow the obvious path through the plantations for some distance until a final steep rise leads to a stile on the edge of the broad summit plateau. A short walk brings you to the remains of the Jubilee Tower.

This was built in 1810 to commemorate the 50th year of the reign of King George III. A ceremony, attended by over 3,000 people who made the long walk to the summit, was held on October 25th and included "most of the nobility and gentry in Denbighshire and Flintshire."

Designed in the Egyptian style, it was originally intended to reach a height of 150 feet. The plans were never fully carried out however, and the structure that was built collapsed in 1862 following a series of storms. Attempts were made to restore the tower in 1887 for Queen Victoria's Golden Jubilee but renovations were a failure and the present structure is all that remains.

All that is of interest here today are the four engraved panoramas which depict highlights from one of the most extensive views in the Clwydian Hills.

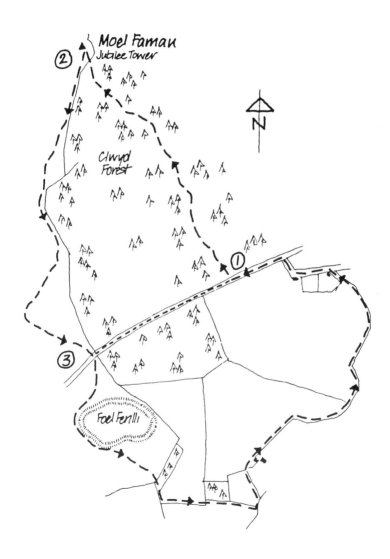

Following Offa's Dyke Path below Foel Fenlli

2. Leave the tower at its southern corner and take the Offa's Dyke Path which heads due south along the broad ridge with conifer woods to the left and an extensive view over the Vale of Clwyd to your right. Continue to the hill road below Foel Fenlli.

3. To shorten the walk turn left here and follow the road back to point **1**. Alternatively, bear diagonally-right up the steep slopes of Foel Fenlli following the Offa's Dyke signs which take you around the western perimeter of the Iron Age hill fort crowning the summit.

This is one of the most impressive hill forts on the Clwydian Hills. The earthworks which enclose the hilltop rise to 35 feet above the outer ditch in places and enclose an area almost ¾ mile across.

Within the defences, remains of over 30 hut circles, along with fragments of fifth century Romano-British pottery and coins have been found. Two returned entrances originally gave access to the fort and a wooden palisade would have topped the ramparts.

At over 1,600 feet, Foel Fenlli commands a wide panorama, particularly to the west where smooth, sheep grazed hillsides drop steeply to the greenery of the Vale of Clwyd. The little market town of Ruthin fits comfortably into this agricultural landscape, while further west the flatness of the Denbigh Moors contrasts sharply with the serrated peaks of Snowdonia which peep over the horizon. To the north and south, the graceful curves of the Clwydian Hills rise and fall, while to the east lies the flatness of the Cheshire Plain.

On the southern side of the hill, descend steeply to a pass with a young conifer plantation to the left. Cross a stile to enter grazing fields and bear left along the fence in the field corner heading towards a small wood. Continue beside the trees at first, then beside the wall.

In the corner of the field leave Offa's Dyke Path which bears right here, instead turn left over a stile and follow a farm track to Fron Hen, a large stone-built farmhouse on the hillside. Keep to the left of the farm and join a track which contours the hillside beside the wall for about 1 mile.

Drop to a lane beside a cottage, turn left and at a T junction turn left again returning to point **1.**

8. Llanarmon-yn-Ial

Distance: *4¼ or 6½ miles*

Start: *Begin at The Raven Inn in the village of Llanarmon-yn-Ial. This is situated on the B5431, 2½ miles south of Llanferres between Mold and Ruthin.*
Grid ref. 191 562 (Landranger 116, Pathfinder 788).

The Route

1. Turn right by The Raven Inn (with the church to your left) and after about 100 yards look for a signed footpath on the right between cottages. After a few yards cross a stile and bear half-left through the centre of the field (aim for a large quarry on the hillside). Follow the path through two smaller fields and after the third stile bear right around the field edge to a stile in the far corner by a caravan (stream to the right).

Follow a well worn footpath through a small field to where a footbridge leads over the stream. Beyond the bridge, follow a track for about 30 yards before turning left onto a narrow footpath. Turn left at the lane and after about 500 yards (just beyond a quarry on the right) a narrow green lane on the left leads down to the stream again. A footbridge leads over the water and a rise is made to a quiet lane.

2. Cross the lane and take the track opposite to "Cyfnant Uchaf". After about 100 yards turn right over a stile and rise to "Tyddyn Uchaf", a smaller farmhouse high on the hillside. Bear right just before the house and aim for a solitary tree on the skyline. Beyond this turn half-left and descend a steeply sloping field which drops into an attractive little valley. A stile on the left at the bottom of the slope confirms that you are still on the right of way.

Cut through the fields straight ahead aiming for a grey farmhouse near a conifer wood. Keep to the left of the house and look for a stile beside the outbuildings. This leads onto a footpath which bears left at first before turning sharp right to rise through the trees.

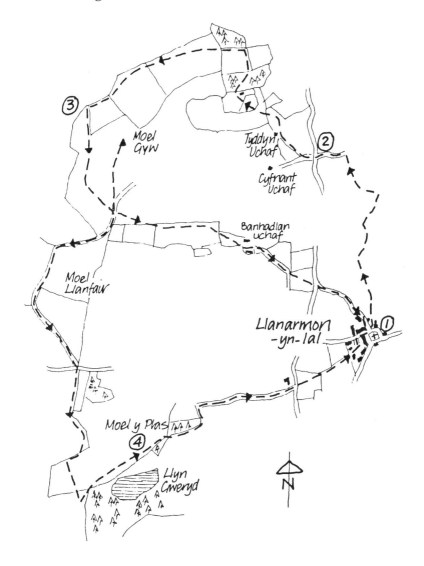

Keep left at a fork to emerge in fields once more at the top of the rise. Follow the path straight ahead and just before a stile leads into a second conifer wood, turn left along the fence. In the field corner pass into the next large field (no stile) and contour the hillside aiming for the lower right corner of the field with a fine view northwards to Moel Eithinen and Foel Fenlli.

Go through a gate in the corner of the field and stay beside the fence. Ignore a second gate on the right, instead continue rising to the shoulder of Moel Gyw where a gate leads onto Offa's Dyke Path.

3. Turn left here and follow a broad path which contours the hillside.

Where the path forks on the pass between Moel Gyw and Moel Llanfair, turn sharp left and follow a narrow footpath

Following Offa's Dyke Path below Moel Gyw

which cuts through the heather to the triangulation pillar on the summit of Moel Gyw. It must be noted that this particular section is not a public right of way, although there is a footpath present and there seems to be no objection to walkers using it.

This little excursion is well worth while and the panorama from the summit is one of the finest on the Clwydian Hills. The view to the west is dominated by the Vale of Clwyd, with its rich green fields and oak lined hedgerows. The focal point of this southern end of the valley is the market town of Ruthin, built on a rise adjacent to the castle and arranged around St Peter's Square.

The most prominent feature from here is undoubtedly the tall broach spire of St Peter's church, added during restoration work carried out in 1856-9. The main fabric of the church is fourteenth century and originally housed a small community of monks. Perhaps because of this, parts of the church were demolished after the Dissolution. Inside is a fine carved and panelled roof said to have been presented by Henry VII in gratitude to the men of North Wales who fought beside him on Bosworth Field in 1485.

The rest of the town is a pleasant mix of period styles with several buildings dating back to the fifteenth and sixteenth centuries. Of particular note is the Old Court House, originally built in 1401 with remains of the town gibbet still visible.

The nearby castle was originally built in the thirteenth century during the reign of Edward I. Parts of the original fabric remain but the majority is modern and now houses a hotel.

Edward I gave Ruthin to the Grey family following his conquest of Wales in 1283 and it was still in their ownership when Owain Glyndwr burned much of the town along with St Asaph cathedral in 1401. Glyndwr's famous rebellion is said to have been triggered by a minor quarrel with Lord Grey over land near Glyndyfrdwy.

Retrace your steps to the pass where you have two options. For a shorter round continue from paragraph **A** or for a longer walk go to paragraph **B**.

A. Look for a narrow footpath which bears left through the heather to a ladder stile. This path leaves a recently built agricultural road beside a large boundary stone separating the parishes of Llanarmon-yn-Ial, Llanfair Dyffryn and Llanbedr. As you enter grazing fields, bear half-right to a second stile beside a gate. Turn left along the fence now and walk along the crest of a rounded ridge with an attractive little valley to your left and Llanarmon-yn-Ial immediately ahead.

As you begin to drop bear half-right to a stile, then cut through a small field towards a farmhouse. After a stile, bear left around the garden to join an access road leading to the farm (Banhadlen Uchaf). Turn left along the road and where it bears right, a stile straight ahead marks the field path back to Llanarmon-yn-Ial. Bear half-right through the field and enter a lane beside a small chapel. Continue straight ahead here and return to Llanarmon-yn-Ial.

B. Follow a recently built agricultural road which bears right down the hill. At the bottom of the slope an Offa's Dyke waymark directs you leftwards onto a second track which again contours the hillside to a gap in the hills. Cross a farm road here and take a steeper path opposite which rises to Moel-y-plas.

At the top of the slope follow the path through the heather and bilberries beside the fence until a stile leads into grazing fields. Turn right for about 25 yards, then bear left down a sloping field. Cross a stile at the bottom of the slope, turn left immediately and cross a second stile at the edge of woods. Follow the path through a large field with the waters of Llyn Gweryd to the right.

The village of Llanarmon-yn-Ial

4. Beyond the lake look for a stile amongst the trees on the right and make a short descent to a farm track. Turn left here and follow the track for some distance. At a T junction beyond a large farmhouse on the left (Plas Llanarmon), take a field path directly ahead, signposted "Llanarmon-yn-Ial". Bear half-left through the centre of the field, then keep to field edges eventually entering a modern housing estate (Maes Ial). Turn left, then left again and at a T junction turn right returning to The Raven Inn.

9. Moel-y-Waun & Craigfechan

Distance: *5¼ miles.*

Start: Begin the walk at The Three Pigeons public house in the little village of Craigfechan. This lies about 2 miles southeast of Ruthin on the B5429.
Grid ref. 147 544 (Landranger 116, Pathfinder 788).

The Route

1. Turn right along the lane passing The Three Pigeons and take the first turning on the left beside the stream. Almost immediately, bear left onto a narrower footpath which rises to a track. Bear left and follow the track to a stile with a large white house to the left. Cross the stile and keep beside the wall with woods on your left and a steep wooded hillside to your right.

Just beyond a small quarry to your right and with a small field immediately ahead, turn sharp right onto a faint footpath which climbs through the trees to the top of a little limestone ridge.

This elevated platform gives the first clear view of the Vale of Clwyd, whose green fields reach north to the coast at Rhyl and Prestatyn. To the west lie the rounded moors of Mynydd Hiraethog which hold the blanket conifers of the Clocaenog Forest. In the shelter of the valley lie the peaceful settlements of Llanfair Dyffryn Clwyd and the market town of Ruthin, burnt by Owain Glyndwr in the fifteenth century after his famous quarrel with Lord Grey.

The rock outcrop which we stand on is part of the belt of limestone which runs all along the North Wales border, giving rise to several small cave systems. Though nothing here can rival the magnificent caverns of Yorkshire and Derbyshire, they have produced some of the earliest evidence of human habitation in Wales. A little further north near Tremeirchion, two caves were excavated in the last century and a number of human bones and flint tools were found along with the remains of several extinct animals such as hyenas, mammoths and woolly rhinoceros.

At the top of the rise keep straight ahead and at the fence turn right. Keep beside the fence until you reach a stile which

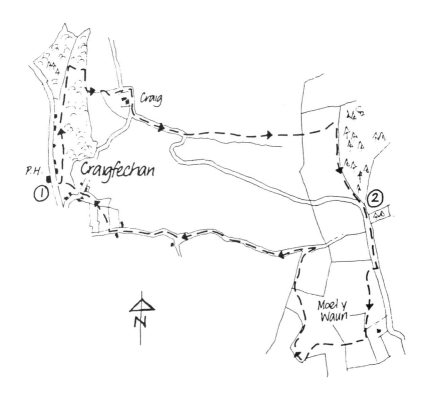

enables you to pass into fields on the left. Part way along the hedge turn right over a second stile then continue with the hedge on your left to reach a narrow lane beside Craig Farm.

Turn right along the lane keeping left at a fork and just before the road bears right over a bridge, turn left over a stile. Follow a well used footpath now which rises through an attractive little valley, bracken covered on its left side.

At the head of the valley, turn right onto Offa's Dyke Path which runs beside a line of conifers on the skyline. Follow this path to the road.

Leaving the lane above Craig Farm

2. Go straight ahead along the lane and at the top of the rise, a stile on the right leads into fields once more. The grass covered remains of an old wall curve left from here; follow this, then keep beside a fence until you are just above a white farmhouse on your left. In the corner of the field climb over the fence (no stile) and turn left along the field edge again. After about 30 yards turn sharp right and rise through the centre of the field to a stile on the skyline.

Beyond the stile descend the hillside bearing half-right to a gate which leads into grazing fields. Descend the field bearing right to join a farm track which runs beside the wall. Turn right here and follow the track for some distance.

After bearing right near a small group of trees, turn sharp left onto a second track beyond a gate. This track descends between grazing fields for some distance.

Keep right at a fork and turn right down a narrow lane by a small cottage. Follow the lane for some distance before turning right over a stile just beyond a white bungalow on the right ("Bryn Dybyn"). Cut diagonally-left through the field to a stile and footbridge in the bottom corner. Keep to the field edge in the following field and look for a stile which leads through a garden to a lane. Turn right, then immediately left onto a short access road. After about 100 yards, turn left onto a footpath which descends beside the stream and at the road turn right and return to point **1.**

10. World's End

Distance: *6½ miles*

Start: Begin the walk at World's End. Parking is not permitted here but a small car park has been provided part way up the lane on the left.
Grid ref. 233 484 (Landranger 117, Pathfinder 806).

The Route

1. Turn left out of the car park and follow the lane up the hill and out of the woods. Turn right almost immediately onto a signed footpath which runs parallel to the woods.

This has been worn into a broad track and a number of narrower paths bear right. Ignore these, instead continue for some distance to a prominent junction of paths (by a small lone pine tree) and turn right onto another broad path. After about 500 yards, at a point where you come close to the conifers, look for a faint path on the right which drops steeply into the trees. A stile takes you over the fence and a steep rocky path leads through the woods and into the little gorge of World's End below the terraced crags of Craig y Forwyn.

This picturesque little valley is formed by the meeting of Craig yr adar and the steep white terraces of Craig y Forwyn, haunt of rock climbers on warm summer evenings. Craig y Forwyn is also known as "The Maiden's Rock", recalling the fate of a young girl who is said to have thrown herself from the crags after a failed love affair.

The crags are composed of carboniferous limestone laid down in ancient seas millions of years ago and thrust upwards by earth movements in more recent times. A rich collection of lime loving plants are found here in stark contrast to the acid vegetation of the plateau above.

2. At the road turn left and after about 30 yards take the (signed) Offa's Dyke Path, also on the left. Follow the path through the trees to emerge on the scree covered hillsides below the terraced crags of Eglwyseg Mountain. Follow the well worn footpath which traverses the hillside below the crags.

As you traverse these scree covered slopes you are treated to a fine view of the beautiful green valley of Eglwyseg Glen. The lush green fields of the valley floor and the softer hillsides to the right contrast sharply with the stoney slopes and near vertical crags which form an unbroken wall for over three miles and provide rock climbers with some of the hardest climbs in northeast Wales.

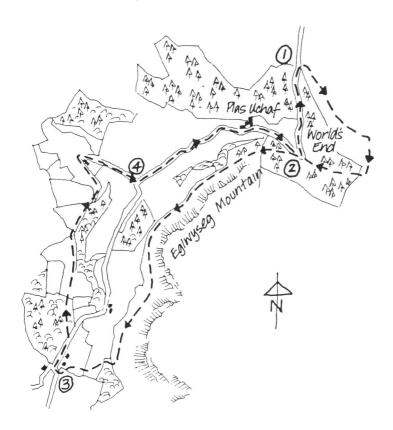

After about 1 mile and just before you curve into the second cove of crags (above a group of farms in the valley) look for a well hidden stile in the fence a little way down the scree on the right. In the summer months this may be hidden amongst the trees so look carefully. Beyond the stile, drop to a farm track, turn right and enter a large field. Turn left down the field (as indicated by a waymark) and aim for a gap in the lower hedge. Walk directly through the second field to the lower left-hand corner and turn left over the stile. After a few yards bear right through a gate to emerge in a quiet lane.

3. Turn right over a stone bridge and follow the lane with woods on the left. About 300 yards along the lane bear left over a stile into the woods and follow a narrow path which rises diagonally through the trees. After leaving the woods the path continues to rise with fine views of the crags of Eglwyseg Mountain to your right.

At the top of the rise enter a field, turn right and walk along the field edge to a gate. Beyond the gate there are two tracks, take the track to the right which descends gradually to a small farmhouse then bears sharp right. Follow the track to the road.

4. Turn left and follow the narrow lane back to World's End.

Just before World's End is the Elizabethan half-timbered manor house of Plas Uchaf, built on the site of the twelfth century hunting lodge of Owain ap Cadwgan. It was to this remote spot that Owain is said to have brought the beautiful wife of Gerald of Pembroke whom he had recently kidnapped. This resulted in a small war which, because of her success at the king's court involved not only her husband, but also Henry I (who is said to have fathered one of her numerous children). Owain was forced to flee to Ireland for a while leaving his father to make peace with Henry which resulted in the loss of half his lands. After his father's death Owain returned and was confirmed Prince of Powys in 1114. He was killed two

Following Offa's Dyke Path below Eglwyseg Mountain

years later while on the king's business by supporters of Gerald of Pembroke.

The most well know occupant of the house was Colonel John Jones, brother-in-law of Oliver Cromwell and one of the signatories of Charles I's death warrant. He is said to have loved the house so much that he risked his life to come here while in hiding prior to his execution on the return of Charles II.

Where the stream flows over the lane below the crags of Craig y Forwyn, either retrace the outward journey up the gorge and back over the moors or bear left up the lane to the car park at point **1**.

Eglwyseg Glen and the crags of Eglwyseg Mountain

11. Llantysilio Mountain

Distance: *5¼ miles*

Start: Begin the walk at the tiny hamlet of Rhewl, 3 miles west of Llangollen on the northern the banks of the River Dee (Afon Dyfrdwy). Park opposite the little red brick chapel. *Grid ref. 183 450 (Landranger 116 & 125, Pathfinder 805).*

The Route

1. Cross the road and follow the narrow lane which rises beside the chapel. After a few yards bear right onto a short track with a white cottage on the right. A gate behind the cottage leads onto a footpath which runs beside a stream. Follow the footpath until a footbridge on the right leads over the stream and you can climb the steep hillside by means of a zigzaging footpath which rises through the trees.

At the top of the bank ignore a stile immediately ahead, instead, bear left following a faint path beside the fence and enter grazing fields by a gate. Keep to the right here and rise a short distance to a large metal gate. Beyond the gate bear left onto a faint farm track and after crossing a stile beside a second gate, bear right up the bank to follow the right of way beside a conifer wood.

At the edge of the trees a gate leads onto the open moors and fine views of the Dee valley begin to open out below. Continue straight ahead beside the fence and bear left onto a track. After a few yards turn right over a stile and rise diagonally right up the hillside following a broad grassy path. At the top of the rise bear left and walk beside the trees again.

As you break out onto the open moors you begin to get the benefit from the height you have gained. Below, the River Dee meanders through the lovely Glyndyfrdwy surrounded by neat, sheep grazed fields and small woods which rise gracefully to the heather covered slopes of Llantysilio Mountain.

It was in this beautiful valley that Owain Glyndwr lived until his rise to fame as the fifteenth century Welsh rebel leader and folk hero. Surprisingly, his journey to fame was triggered by a relatively minor incident—a quarrel over a small plot of land with his neighbour, Lord Grey of Ruthin. Grey it seems, was a royal favourite and managed to get Glyndwr branded a traitor.

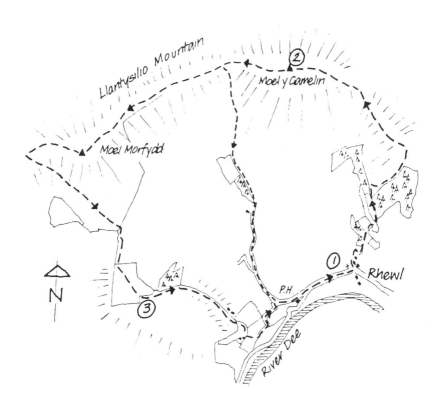

At a time of unrest, with much of Wales suspicious of the new king (Henry IV) who had obtained the crown by usurping Richard II and in the face of such apparent injustice, Glyndwr's countrymen were quick to support him proclaiming him "Prince of Wales".

With his men behind him he embarked on a series of raids and skirmishes which included the burning of both St Asaph Cathedral and the Ruthin estate of Lord Grey. During this campaign his ability to disappear into the hills with his armies and appear again in another location with such speed gave rise to the belief that he possessed magical powers. Henry tried to suppress the uprising but Glyndwr had gained the support of the powerful Sir Edmund Mortimer, Earl of Northumberland who was soon to become his son-in-law.

After failing to take the king's castles at Caernarfon and Harlech in 1401, he won a decisive battle on the slopes of Plynlymon and in 1404 managed to bribe a mutinous garrison into surrendering Harlech Castle. He now had a headquarters and moved his entire family into the safety of the castle where they remained for four years.

Glyndwr almost achieved his dream of a separate Welsh kingdom before his fortunes changed. Harlech fell, his supporters quickly left his side and by 1409, just nine years after his quarrel with Lord Grey, it was all over. He lived as an outlaw for many years refusing a pardon from Henry V and died in obscurity at an unknown location in the hills.

As the path levels off near the spoil heaps of the Berwyn Slate Quarries, bear left and follow a good path (with the slag heaps on your right) to the summit of Moel y Gamelin. *Please note:* the route over Moel Morfydd and Moel y Gamelin is a permissive footpath only. Please respect the landowner's good will and keep to the recognised route.

From here on a clear day the panorama is one of the most extensive in northeast Wales. To the north, the Vale of Clwyd is

Moel y Gamelin from Moel Morfydd

laid out like a vast green carpet bordered to the east by the shapely sheep grazed slopes of the Clwydian Hills and on the west by the flat uplands of the Denbigh Moors. Further west the pointed tops of Snowdonia are visible, while to the south the Berwyns rise above the Dee valley where Henry II met defeat in 1169. To the west, the view is dominated by the limestone crags of Eglwyseg Mountain which rise steeply above the Vale of Llangollen.

2. From the summit a steep descent (west) takes you to a pass crossed by several tracks.

To shorten the walk, turn left here onto a broad track then fork right and follow the bridleway beside a wood to join a lane by Ty 'n-y-mynydd. Follow the lane to the Sun Inn. Alternatively, continue along the ridge making a final steep rise to the triangulation pillar on Moel Morfydd.

Continue west from Moel Morfydd and make a second steep descent. Where the path levels out there are several tracks; turn sharp left here and join a prominent track which contours the hillside below the summit.

Lower down the track bears sharp right; continue straight ahead here on a less distinct path. At a fence turn right and follow it to the field corner. Turn left over the fence here (no stile) then bear right along the edge of grazing fields. The right of way cuts through the fields at the next corner, but it seems easier to stay this side of the fence until you reach a point where four fences meet. Pass into the field immediately ahead and bear diagonally-left aiming to the right of a small conifer wood.

3. At the far side of the field cross a stream and bear left over a stile in the fence. The path runs parallel to the stream, then beside a small wood before descending steadily beside the wall. Just above a farm on your left, bear left onto a track and after about 60 yards turn left over the fence (no stile) and drop to a second track with old outbuildings on the left. Turn right here and after about 250 yards turn left over a stile in the fence. Drop to a farm track, turn left and continue to a narrow lane beyond a gate.

Turn right along the lane and after passing over a stream, rise to a T junction. A right turn here takes you to the Sun Inn, a delightful old inn and a welcome pint. From the Sun Inn continue along the lane back to point **1.** at Rhewl.

12. Horseshoe Pass

Distance: *5½ miles*

Start: There is ample parking at the top of the Horseshoe Pass near the cafe & gift shop.
Grid ref. 193 481 (Landranger 116, Pathfinder 805).

The Route

1. Immediately to the north of the cafe and gift shop the old road to Pentre-dwfr leaves the A542 and passes behind the restaurant before dropping steeply into the valley. Follow this road for about 75 yards before bearing left across the grass to a large gate (ignore an earlier stile on the left). Pass through the gate and follow a grassy path which contours the hillside descending slightly. Further on the path is contained between earth banks and can be very wet.

Where the path approaches a house, go through the first gate, then bear left to a second gate which leads onto the hillside again. Follow a rising path beside the fence for some distance now.

2. After about ¾ mile you reach a high shoulder and the path levels. Join a broad grassy track at a T junction and turn right down the hill passing ruined farm buildings on the right. A little further on, two large metal gates cross the path and about 50 yards beyond this, there are two field gates on the right. Go through the second gate, turn half-left and cut diagonally through the centre of the field. Look for a stile in the fence on your right after about 200 yards. Turn left immediately after the stile and pass through a metal field gate into a large field. Follow a faint track through the centre of the field aiming for a small quarry.

The contrast in the landscape to the right and left here is due to the underlying geology. The smooth flowing contours to the right are the result of slates and mudstones, which explains the presence of the small quarries nearby along with the larger workings on the Llantysilio hills; while the dramatic crags and screes of Eglwyseg Mountain are composed of carboniferous limestone.

At the far end of the field a gate leads onto a track with the small quarry to your right. Follow the track straight ahead and descend with woods on your right and a fine view of Eglwyseg Glen and the crags of Craig Arthur to the left.

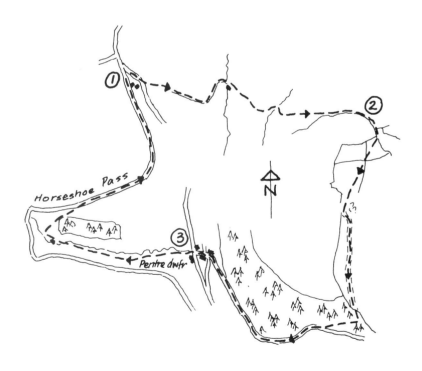

The Horseshoe Pass

Lower down a gate leads into woods and the track continues, bearing sharp right after 100 yards or so. At a junction of tracks keep straight ahead on the main track and continue to the lane. Turn right passing a farm ("Dergoed") on the left and continue along the lane for about 1 mile to the houses and cottages of Pentre-dwfr. Turn right at the first T junction and walk up the lane to a second T junction.

This lane is known as the "Old Horseshoe Pass Road" and was the original road over the hills to Llandegla before being replaced by the present Horseshoe Pass road (A542), built as a Turnpike in 1811. This new road avoided the steep gradients which were both difficult and dangerous for coaches and enabled the nearby quarries to transport slate more efficiently.

3. Directly opposite there is a small bus shelter with a signed footpath to the left. Follow the footpath beside the stream then enter fields by a stile after about 100 yards or so. Keep right along the field edge and pass into the second field by a large metal gate. Walk directly through the following field parallel to the stream, until a stile takes you onto a bracken covered bank. The path is now well worn and can easily be followed to the head of the valley keeping the stream to your right.

Just before a ruined farmhouse, a footbridge leads over the stream on the right before bearing left up the bank to a gate adjacent to the house. Keep straight ahead through the bracken and curve right keeping close to the field edge. Shortly, a stile leads into a small rock-strewn field. Turn right and after about 20 yards a faint footpath on the left rises diagonally up the bank. At the top of the rise walk straight ahead to an old gate with farm buildings to the left. An overgrown footpath takes a diagonal line through the bracken to reach the road and a fine view of the Horseshoe Pass.

Turn right and either follow the road back to the cafe, or take one of the footpaths opposite and across the lower flanks of Moel y Faen.

The slate quarries at the top of the pass were begun about 1802 by Sir Watkin Williams Wynn and were one of the reasons for the building of the Horseshoe Pass road. With increased production in the 1850s came a tramway linking the quarries to the Llangollen/ Ellesmere Canal. The heyday came in the latter half of the nineteenth century but by the turn of the twentieth century demand for slate was in decline. Production finally ceased in the 1950s although the Berwyn Slate Quarry is still worked on a small scale for decorative stone.

13. Valle Crucis Abbey

Distance: *5 miles*

Start: There is free parking available in a large picnic area near the Chain Bridge Hotel, 1½ miles upstream from Llangollen. This is situated just off the B5103 signed to Llantysilio and Rhewl. Enter the car park through the upper entrance just past the outdoor education centre.
Grid ref. 198 433 (Landranger 125, Pathfinder 805).

The Route

1. Leave the car park by the higher entrance and turn right along the lane signed to "Velvet Hill and Valle Crucis Abbey ¾ m". Walk past the outdoor education centre and at the first lane on the left turn left onto the signed footpath to "Velvet Hill Valle Crucis Abbey". Follow the path through the trees, cross a stile and keep right on a well worn path which contours the hillside. A little further on where the path forks, take the lower signed path to "Valle Crucis Abbey". A stile at the bottom of the slope leads onto the road. Turn left here and just after Abbey Dingle Nursing Home, cross the road to a kissing gate which leads into a small field. Walk directly through the field with the Abbey directly ahead to a second kissing which leads onto a track. Turn left along the track and the entrance to the Abbey is just a few yards away on the right.

The Abbey was built around 1200 by Madog ap Gruffydd of Castell Dinas Bran who ruled Powys from 1191-1236 and takes its name from the nearby Pillar of Eliseg, which had been erected three centuries earlier and was evidently a well known local landmark when the abbey was built (Valle Crucis means "Valley of the Cross"). It was run by monks of the Cistercian order who

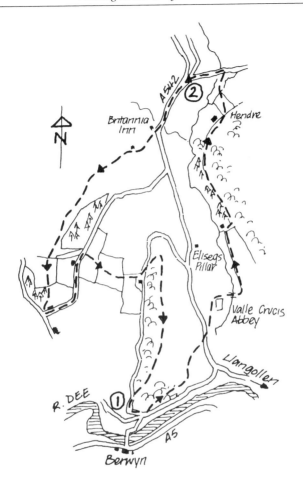

sought out remote locations such as this where they could be self sufficient. It became the burial place of its founder and his son Gruffydd and is reputedly the resting place of Iolo Goch, the celebrated poet who became Owain Glyndwr's court bard.

The present ruins date from the late thirteenth century when the abbey was extensively rebuilt following a fire. Its ruinous state today is largely due to Henry VIII's Dissolution of the Monasteries in the sixteenth century, although large portions of the building *remain, along with extensive foundations to give us an impression of its former glory. It was scheduled as an Ancient Monument in 1933 although it remained in private ownership until 1949. Extensive repairs have been carried out and a series of wall-mounted interpretation panels explain various aspects of the ruins.*

On leaving the Abbey site turn right through a large gate into a caravan site. Keep right along the access road and where this bends left, walk straight ahead to a footbridge over the stream. Beyond the bridge steps take you up the bank and a sign at the top of the slope directs you either right to "Llangollen" or left to "Tan y Fron". Turn left here and keep to the field edge. Immediately before the farm climb a ladder stile and turn right up a short track to a gate and second

Valle Crucis Abbey

stile. After the stile turn left onto a good footpath which should be followed for some distance.

After the woods on your left give way to open fields you pass a small cottage on the left ("Hendre") and just beyond this there is a stile into fields, also on the left. Cross the stile and walk diagonally-right to a stile in the lower right-hand corner. Beyond the stile bear right along a steep bank overlooking a valley and stream to a stile which leads into a quiet lane. Turn left up the hill and at a T junction turn left again.

2. At the main road turn left and after about 300 yards turn right to pass through the car park of The Britannia Inn. Look for an access road directly ahead which rises from the car park (footpath sign) and follow this to a large house on the hillside. Immediately before the house, turn left and follow a signed path around the house and garden to emerge on the open hillside after a stile. Turn left beside the fence at first, then contour the open hillside until you come to a stile in the fence on your right. Go over the stile and continue to contour with woods down to your left until you come to a grassy track descending the hillside. Bear left along the track and drop to a large metal gate with a stile beside it. Go through the gate and walk directly through the following field to join a track with woods on the right. Follow the track to the road.

Turn left here and walk along the lane for about 600 yards. Just beyond a white house on the left (Maesyrychen Uchaf) turn right through a gate into fields. Cut through the centre of the field to a footbridge over a stream. Beyond the bridge, bear half-right towards a stone cottage. A stile beside a cattle trough leads into the final field before the house. A stile to the left of the garden takes you onto the access drive. Turn left here and left again at the lane. After about 50 yards bear right off the road to a stile which leads onto the open hillside.

Take the path to the left until you round the hillside to overlook the valley with the Pillar of Eliseg below.

The Pillar of Eliseg one of the most important Dark Age monuments in the Welsh borders. The pillar is in fact the shaft of an inscribed stone cross from the ninth century which commemorates Eliseg, Prince of Powys. Originally about twelve feet high, the cross stands on the site of an earlier burial mound and was erected about AD 850.

During the Civil War it was thrown down and defaced by Parliamentarian troops but remains of the shaft were later re-erected. Despite this treatment, the Latin inscription, which is now unreadable, was recorded and translated by Edward Llwyd in 1696 and was found to recall the glories of the royal house of Powys. The inscription tells us that the pillar was erected by Cyngen in honour of his great-grandfather, Eliseg Prince of Powys who rescued the kingdom of Powys from the hand of the English "with fire and sword."

Eliseg was a contemporary of Offa, the English ruler of Mercia who constructed the mighty earthwork along the Welsh border which today bears his name. The inscription also lists Eliseg's ancestry back to Vortigern, the fourth century British high king whose attempt to recruit mercenaries from the continent resulted in the Saxon invasion of Britain and Vortigern's reputed exile to a lonely valley on the slopes of Yr Eifl in northern Lleyn.

Turn sharp right now and follow the crest of the rounded ridge over several tops. The final little summit overlooks the River Dee and gives fine views in all directions. A good path descends the southern side of the hill to reach a lane on the right. Turn left and follow the lane back to the picnic area which will be on your right.

14. Castell Dinas Bran & The Panorama Walk

Distance: *5 miles*

Start: Begin the walk at Llangollen's main car park situated in Market Street, just off Castell Street which leads down to the bridge.
Grid ref. 215 420 (Landranger 117, Pathfinder 806).

The Route

1. Bear right out of the car park and at the end of the road turn left following Castell Street northwards over the Dee bridge.

This ancient bridge has spanned the river for over seven centuries and is thought to have been built during the reign of Henry I and later widened by John Trevor, Bishop of St Asaph, in 1345. It seems likely that the town grew around this crossing although Llangollen's present size and form is mainly due to a short period of prosperity from the wool-trade which flourished here for a while.

Today tourism keeps the local economy alive and one of the town's main attractions is the world famous International Eisteddfod. Originally started by a group of enthusiasts on a much smaller scale, it has expanded to become one of Wales' major events. During the festival, music groups and enthusiasts from around the world descend on the town until its tiny streets are almost swamped. Later these crowds will be housed in one of the largest marquees in the world specially designed for the event.

This is not the only Eisteddfod in Wales, nor was it the first. They have been held in Wales at least since the Middle Ages and

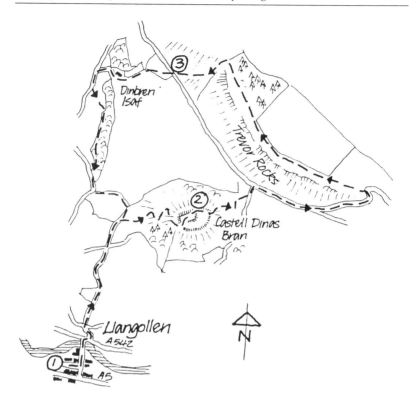

before that similar gatherings at which bardic contests took place would always have been a part of Welsh culture. The word itself means simply "to sit" and is taken from the verb "eistedd". Thus, an Eisteddfod is simply a sitting or "gathering".

Another event which draws in both spectators and participants from around the country is the canoeing championships which use the fast flowing waters of the River Dee at several points around the town.

Of more local interest is the Llangollen Steam Railway which has been restored by a group of enthusiasts. You can now travel through one of Wales' prettiest valleys in traditional style on one of the restored locomotives.

Turn right opposite Bridge End Hotel, then after a few yards bear left up Wharf Hill and cross the Shropshire Union Canal. Just beyond the canal, an enclosed footpath continues straight ahead at a T junction. At the end of the path cross a metalled lane and continue to climb through a small field beside the hedge. A gate in the top corner leads onto an unmetalled access road; follow this and keep straight ahead at a crossroads. At the end of the lane a gate leads onto the hillside and a sign, "Castell Dinas Bran" directs you half-right. After a short dip a steepening path takes you up neat, sheep grazed slopes to the crumbling ruins which crown the highest point.

It is hard to picture a more magnificent setting for a castle than this almost fairy tale hilltop. Look down from the walls at the tiny figures climbing the steep hillside and you will soon see why the site was chosen. Although today the walls have almost disappeared, enough of the structure remains to form a picture of its size and layout. Part of a passageway in the wall on the east side and the remains of the Great Hall to the south can still be identified. Outside the walls, a series of earlier Bronze Age earthworks also enclose the hilltop.

The origin of the castle is not known for sure but it is thought to have been built to replace an earlier stronghold by Gruffydd ap Madog following his fathers death in 1160. As the new Prince of Powys he was only too well aware of the constant threat from across the nearby English border where Norman Marcher Lords waited for their chance to conquer his lands. As a result, he made an alliance with Owain Gwynedd and Rhys ap Gruffydd of Deheubarth.

This new threat soon had Henry II gathering his forces and marching west to meet a strong Welsh army assembled at Corwen. For some reason he chose to march over the Berwyn Mountains by way of Glyn Ceiriog instead of the Vale of Llangollen and it was here that he met with a small force of lightly armed Welsh archers who harassed his army for some time almost killing Henry in one skirmish at Bronygarth below Chirk Castle. These tactics and the appalling weather encountered on the featureless summit of the Berwyns combined to force Henry into a humiliating retreat without even engaging the main Welsh forces. During the retreat Henry took revenge on his captives by tearing out their eyes; among them were the sons of Owain and Rhys.

Despite this victory for the Welsh, Gruffydd decided to pay homage to Henry in 1175 and peace followed until his death in 1191 when his son, Madog ap Gruffydd, replaced him. It was Madog who built the nearby Valle Crucis Abbey in 1201 and reputedly acted as go-between in an important meeting between King John and Llywelyn the Great.

Castell Dinas Bran from the lane below Trevor Rocks

In 1236 he died and was buried at the abbey and seceded by his son, confusingly called Gruffydd ap Madog. In the unrest which followed Llywelyn's death in 1240 he seems to have been unable to decide where his allegiance lay, although he finally joined Llywelyn (II) in an ill-fated rebellion with Simon de Montfort who perished soon afterwards at Evesham.

Gruffydd died in 1269 and was followed by his son who died just nine years later; perhaps defending Dinas Bran during one of Edward I's early Welsh campaigns. His two young sons were put into the guardianship of Earl Warren and Earl Mortimer who are said to have drowned them in the River Dee beneath the arches of the recently completed Holt bridge in order to take over their lands. Dinas Bran fell for the last time in 1283 during Edward's final crushing of Wales although it continued to have tenants until 1495 when the last owner, Sir William Stanley from Chirk Castle, was executed for his part in a rebellion against Henry VII.

In the following century the castle's only occupant is reported to have been an eagle who fiercely attacked anyone who tried to approach its crumbling walls.

2. A well marked path descends the eastern slopes of the hill, with a fine view of the Dee valley and Telford's multi arched aqueduct in the distance, to join a narrow lane below the limestone terraces of Trevor Rocks. Turn left here then right at a T junction after a few yards. Follow the lane which contours the hillside and keep left where the lane forks. After a sharp left-hand bend bear left onto a permissive path signposted, "Panorama". At first follow a faint track which rises to a gate, then keep left beside the fence and walk along the skyline with a fine view of the Vale of Llangollen dominated by Castell Dinas Bran to the left.

Pass through an area of stunted pines and at a finger post bear left down the hillside. Lower down, the path keeps beside a small stream and at one point you are forced to scramble over wet rocks. Immediately below this, look for a path which bears diagonally-right down the screes to the road. Care should be taken on this section of the route.

3. If you managed to locate the correct path there should be a field gate opposite, or, if you followed the stream down to the road turn right and walk up the lane to find the gate on the left. Enter the field keeping left around the field edge and passing close to an old lime kiln on the left. In the corner of the field bear left onto a faint farm track and follow this through two gates to a farm ("Dinbren Isaf"). The right of way passes through the farmyard to join a quiet lane.

Turn left here and after about 100 yards, enter fields again on the left following the path beside a stream. After a short distance, bear left over a footbridge and continue beside the stream. Where the path appears to enter fields by a large gate, bear half-left to a stile and follow an attractive woodland path with fields on the right. At a farm track continue straight ahead to reach the lane.

Turn left here and where the lane bears right, turn left onto a field path signposted, "Castell Dinas Bran". Keep left around the field edge and in the top corner of the field climb a stile bearing right along the hedge. At the top of the rise a gate leads onto the access track used earlier in the walk to reach the castle. Retrace your steps back to Llangollen.

15. Froncysyllte

Distance: *4¾ miles*

Start: Begin in the village of Froncysyllte which rises steeply above the A5 near Thomas Telford's famous aqueduct. Turn off the A5 into "Methodist Hill" almost opposite the Trevor road (B5434) and rise steeply through the village for ¼ mile. Where the road bends sharp right turn left and park on a small piece of waste ground beside a bungalow," Sunnyside". *Grid ref. 272 410 (Landranger 117, Pathfinder 806).*

The Route

1. Walk down the lane for about 150 yards and look for a signed footpath on the left which rises into woods with a small quarry to the right. Continue through the trees until you are forced to bear right by a steep rock face and at the edge of the woods turn left with a field to the right. At a T junction turn left again and after a few yards join a narrow access road by two cottages ("Pen-y-graig").

Take the bridleway between the two cottages which soon runs beside a large quarry on the left. Just beyond this a small elevated platform provides a fine viewpoint.

In clear weather there is an extensive panorama from here. The flat expanse of the Cheshire Plain extends eastwards to the industry at Stanlow and the sandstone hills at Helsby, Beeston and Peckforton. Occasionally, the Pennines may be visible on the farthest skyline along with the Shropshire hills further south.

Nearer at hand the industrial towns of Acrefair, Ruabon and Cefn sprawl across the lower slopes of Ruabon Mountain, while the rural beauty of the Vale of Llangollen takes us into an altogether different landscape.

The industrial activity of the nearby border towns has had little impact on this landscape of rolling hills, green valleys and pretty market towns. At the head of the valley Llangollen sits astride the River Dee, justifiably regarded as one of North Wales' prettiest towns. Around it are arranged the Llantysilio Hills and the craggy escarpments of Eglwyseg Mountain, while the medieval ruins of Castell Dinas Bran watch over the town from its elevated hilltop.

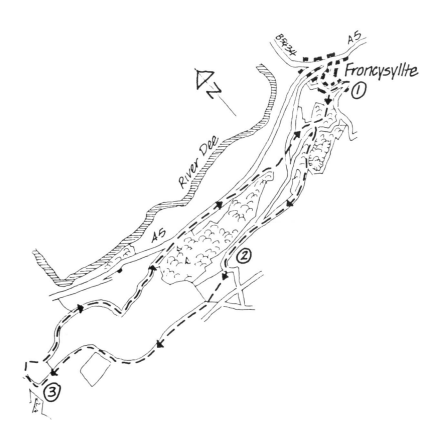

From here the path splits, one branch bears left to a stile in the fence among the trees, while our route continues straight ahead for a few more yards before bearing left to run beside the fence. Low bushes and scrub make progress a little difficult at first but the path soon becomes more established and enclosed on both sides. Continue to the road.

2. Turn left and follow the road to a sharp left-hand bend. A stile on the right here leads into fields. Bear half-right up the bank and cross a large open field aiming for a stile in the fence. This leads onto a track; turn right and follow the track along the hillside for some distance.

3. Where the track begins to drop steeply with woods below and to the left, turn right along the wall.

To the left the hillside falls steeply into Pengwern Vale, a curving 'U' shaped valley originally cut by the River Dee. Although the river takes a different line today, the valley often holds water during heavy rain.

At the Llangollen end of the vale stands Plas Newydd, one of the most well known houses in North Wales. Between 1779 and 1831 it was home to Lady Elanor Charlotte Butler and Miss Sarah Ponsonby, two Irish aristocrats who came be known as the "Ladies of Llangollen".

Their life style and masculine way of dress was a little unconventional for the time and many considered them eccentric although their hospitality was well known. As a result of this, and because Llangollen lay on the stage coach road from London to Holyhead, they played host to many famous individuals including Sir Walter Scott, William Wordsworth, Tennyson and Sheridan.

During their stay at Plas Newydd the ladies transformed the plain stone-built house into something more to their liking. The most notable addition is the large amount of carving probably collected from churches or other houses in the vicinity. In addition there is a large amount of stained glass and Cordovan leather all of which remain.

Their creativity was also extended to the 12 acres of farmland which surrounded the house. This they transformed into a large landscaped garden which include the Cyflmen stream and its valley.

Look for a gap in the wall on the right after about 200 yards. This leads into fields and you pass through the ruins of old farm buildings. Turn right again just beyond the ruins (ignore a more obvious path straight ahead here) and follow a contouring footpath to a gate. Beyond the gate a track runs along the hillside for about 1 mile.

Thomas Telford's aqueduct at Froncysyllte

At the busy A5 turn right and follow the road for about 400 yards. Here a well defined path on the right rises diagonally up the hillside for some distance. At a narrow lane continue straight ahead and after a small field on the left turn left onto a path which soon bears right into a wooded quarry. Retrace the outward journey now.

Froncysyllte's claim to national fame is the nearby aqueduct built by Thomas Telford in the closing years of the eighteenth century. It carries the Shropshire Union Canal over the Dee valley by means of 18 stone piers which rise to over 120 feet. The structure was considered to be one of the great engineering feats of the time and took ten years to complete, opening in 1805. Telford tried a completely new approach here and employed the use of cast iron on a scale previously unthinkable. His idea worked wonderfully though and much of the original work remains, including the mortar between the stones of the masonry piers believed to be a mixture of ox blood and lime.

Shortly after the aqueduct opened, the original concept of a link between the Severn at Shrewsbury and the Dee at Chester was abandoned when it was decided not to complete the last section of the canal between Cefn and Chester. This decision made the entire waterway inviable and its use by commercial craft slowly declined.

Today the waterway is used exclusively by pleasure boats and the section between here and Llangollen, originally the least viable on the entire canal system, is now one of the most popular stretches.

Mara Publications

Mara Publications publish a range walking guides and have the following list to date:

A Walkers Guide to the Wirral Shore Way ISBN 0 9522409 0 4
This describes a linear walk of over 20 miles between Chester and Hoylake following Wirral's old coastline.

Circular Walks along the Sandstone Trail ISBN 0 9522409 2 0
This book gives a complete north-south route description as well as breaking the trail into 12 circular walks.

Circular Walks along the Gritstone Trail and Mow Cop Trail
ISBN 0 9522409 4 7
A route which follows Cheshire's eastern border along the edge of the Peak District. Following the same format as the Sandstone Trail book—a full route description for both trails is combined with 12 circular walks.

Circular Walks in Wirral ISBN 0 9522409 1 2
A collection of 12 circular walks in Wirral.

Coastal Walks around Anglesey ISBN 0 9522409 6 3
15 circular walks around Anglesey's wild and beautiful coast now designated an Area of Outstanding Natural Beauty.

Walking in the Conwy Valley ISBN 0 9522409 7 1
A collection of circular walks centred on the Conwy Valley between Betws y Coed and Llandudno.

All the above books can be obtained from bookshops or direct from the publisher.